The emperor's
palaces and gardens

The blind
emperor

River Jordan

The temple

The suitors

They're lost

THE
GARDENER'S APPRENTICE
A Folktale and Flower Journal

THE GARDENER'S APPRENTICE

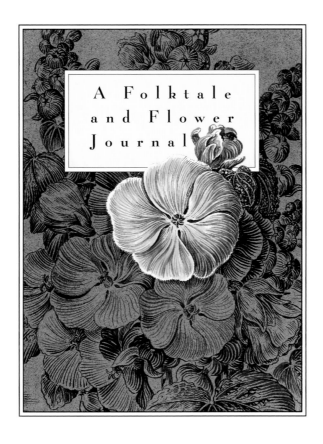

A Folktale
and Flower
Journal

Adapted by Eric Metaxas and Illustrated by Rodica Prato

Creative Editions

Published in 1998 by Creative Editions
123 South Broad Street, Mankato, Minnesota 56001 USA

Creative Editions is an imprint of The Creative Company

Library of Congress Cataloging-in-Publication Data
Metaxas, Eric.
  The gardener's apprentice / by Eric Metaxas; illustrated by Rodica Prato.
  Summary: In this version of a traditional Romanian tale, a boy wise beyond
his years leaves home with a magical horse and has many adventures.
    ISBN 1-56846-154-2
  [1. Fairy tales. 2. Folklore—Romania.] I. Prato, Rodica, ill. II. Title.
PZ8.M55Gar 1997b
392.2'09498—dc21   96-36895

First edition
E D C B A

When the husband got home he gave the apple to his wife.

The Apple

Once upon a time there lived a couple who had no children, only a beautiful white mare. They loved her greatly, for she was all they had to help them bear the hardships of life. But more than anything in the world, this couple longed to have a child. They tried every remedy and took every suggestion, no matter how ridiculous, but nothing seemed to work.

One day, they heard of a sorcerer whose powers were such that he was able to turn water into stones at a glance. The husband quickly went to him and told him their sad tale.

The sorcerer said he knew of something to break the curse over them. Once they had settled on a price, the sorcerer took a blood red apple from his cloak and gave it to the husband. "Your wife alone must eat from this apple," he told the husband. "See that no other living creature eats of it."

When the husband got home he gave the apple to his wife. She took it from his hand with greater joy than she had ever known. When her husband went off to do his work, she sat alone on the doorstep of their humble home, peeled the shining red fruit, and devoured it. Now, the young mare was just then coming up the path to her master's house, for she hoped that they would give her some oats to eat. But when she saw the red and white curls of apple peel lying on the ground at her mistress's feet, she ate them instead, and they tasted sweeter and more delicious than any delicacy.

In a short time, both the woman and the horse became pregnant. After nine months, the woman gave birth to a beautiful male child and the mare to a delicate white foal. When the husband considered this double blessing of the child and the foal, his heart leapt with joy. He proclaimed that, because they had been born together, no one would ride the foal except for his son when he reached the proper age.

And so they baptized their child and cared for him in the way that parents care for an only child. The child grew. When he was a year old, it seemed that he was five and when he reached five years, he seemed to be fifteen. The more he grew, the more handsome he became, and he learned more quickly than anyone in the world.

One day, an idea came into the boy's head and he mounted the young horse and spurred him. The animal, which was now fully grown, leapt about wildly and began to run at a tremendous speed with the boy on its back. In a moment's time, they had disappeared into the distance and were never seen again. When the boy's parents discovered that their son was gone, they looked everywhere for him—behind each cloud and under each rock, to the left and to the right. They spoke to every soul for many miles around, but it was hopeless. He was nowhere to be found.

Perhaps it was because of the restless energy of youth, but when the boy and the horse saw the wide open spaces stretching

One day, an idea came into the boy's head and he mounted the young horse and spurred him.

before them, it never occurred to them to do anything but race toward the horizon as fast as they could. They went further and further from home until the sun set and they both realized that they were in a strange land, quite unlike the place they had left. They were quickly filled with fear, for they didn't know which road would take them back, nor which road had brought them there.

At that moment, the boy began to cry and he longed for his dear parents. The horse, seeing his master's troubled heart, tried to comfort him and together they searched for a place to rest for the night. Finally, their weariness chose a spot for them. And so they lay down to sleep in a ditch by the side of the road, with a starless black sky as their only blanket.

The next day, they walked and walked, but found no shelter or food anywhere. They searched for their footsteps, hoping they could retrace them, but it was useless. Again the boy began to cry and wanted to return to his parents.

"Meanwhile, I will go and find a place for us back in the world of men."

Seeing the hopelessness of their situation, the horse spoke. "Master," he said, "allow me to go and find the way out of this place."

"That's out of the question," the boy replied. "We're in a desolate country, a howling wilderness, without houses or inhabitants. I can't be left here alone."

"Take my bridle," the horse said. "When you need me, only shake it. In a moment, I will return to your side. Meanwhile, I will go and find a place for us back in the world of men." Before the boy had time enough to get bored, the horse had traversed the entire sky and returned, saying he'd found a place where the boy might find employment. He told the boy all that he must do to turn the situation to his advantage. As soon as he heard all this, the boy mounted the horse and they left there as quickly as they'd arrived, seven times faster than the wind itself.

The  Nymphs

At last, they came to the home of three golden-haired nymphs. The nymphs were at first reluctant to take him into their service, but the boy persisted, promising to work hard and be faithful in his duties, until, at last, they agreed. The boy did his work with all his heart and whenever he faced any difficulty he shook the bridle and the horse came to help him.

Now, the horse had learned the secret of the nymphs' powers and so he instructed his master to observe the nymphs' bathing pool carefully, for at a certain time liquid gold would flow there instead of water. He also told him to look for three walnuts which the nymphs kept hidden in the bottom of a chest, and the boy did just as he was told.

One day, when the nymphs had gone out hunting, the boy heard a curious sound of rushing water, louder than any he'd heard before, coming from the bathing pool. The sound filled him with

When he emerged from the golden waters, his hair was so long that it fell below his waist. . . .

fear and by shaking the bridle he summoned his horse. When the horse saw what was happening, he told his master to undress quickly, and then he pushed the boy into the bathing pool with a splash. When he emerged from the golden waters, his hair was so long that it fell below his waist, and it was of a golden color so brilliant that, though the brightness hurt the eyes, one could not bear to look away. Taking the three walnuts, which he'd found earlier, he mounted his horse and set out onto the road.

When he went through the outer gate of the nymphs' house, the house itself started to shriek so loudly that the sound could have pulled the dead from their tombs. The nymphs returned in a moment and quickly saw that their servant was nowhere to be found. They were soon right behind him, but when the horse saw them he galloped faster, as fast as thought itself. In the very moment that the nymphs were about to catch them, they crossed the border of their realm and were safe.

In the very moment that the nymphs were about to catch them, they crossed the border of their realm and were safe.

After some time, the boy and his horse came to the realm of a great Emperor. As before, the horse told the boy just what he must do, in great detail, and once the boy understood perfectly he proceeded to the imperial gardens of the Emperor's palace to ask for employment. In order to conceal his golden locks, he covered his head with a dried cow's bladder, which made him look as bald as a summer melon. Because of this, everyone in the court called him the Bald One.

The gardener took him in and quickly taught him how to plant flower seeds, transplant the young flowers, and care for them. The new apprentice was a surprisingly quick learner, and the gardener was quite impressed. In everything he did, the apprentice became the gardener's right hand.

Three   Bouquets

Now the gardener had grown old in the Emperor's service, and he was an honest man. It was his happy duty each morning to make three beautiful bouquets of flowers, one for each of the Emperor's daughters. One day, feeling ill, he summoned his apprentice to perform this duty, telling him to choose the most beautiful flowers in the garden and to make three bouquets and give them to the Emperor's daughters. So the bald apprentice made three bouquets, one very large, one medium in size, and one small. The large one was made of flowers past their bloom, some of which had begun to wilt slightly and lose their aroma, and this he gave to the eldest daughter. The medium-sized bouquet was made of flowers in full bloom, and this he gave to the middle daughter. The small bouquet of buds just beginning to open he gave to the youngest daughter. As soon as he had presented the three bouquets, he quickly returned to the garden to continue his day's work.

As soon as he had presented the three bouquets, he quickly returned to the garden to continue his day's work.

The daughters were astonished at the three very different bouquets, the two eldest daughters most of all, and they took their flowers to their father. The Emperor immediately summoned the gardener to ask the meaning of the different bouquets, but the gardener quickly cleared his name, explaining that he'd been ill that morning and had sent his apprentice, the Bald One, to bring the flowers.

So they summoned the bald apprentice. When he approached the Emperor, he drew near with great humility and spoke: "Long life to you, most luminous sovereign! When I picked the flowers and arranged the bouquets I only meant well, as God is my witness. I gave each princess the flowers that I thought suited her."

The Emperor looked at the apprentice, who appeared in earnest. The Emperor thought the situation over. His anger disappeared as he came to understand the message in the three bouquets.

His daughters were grown up. He had been remiss in his duties to find husbands for them. It was time they were married.

Later, he sent a bag of gold coins to the apprentice. But the apprentice gave the bag to the gardener and said he had no use for the money, and that he owed everything he had learned about flowers to his master.

The Garden

Not long afterwards, there was a holy day. The Emperor and his court and all of his wisest councillors went to church. Among these was the old gardener. Only the young princess, who was feeling ill, remained in the palace.

Now the apprentice, thinking he was quite alone, took the bridle from inside his clothing, along with the first of the three walnuts. He opened the walnut. It contained a magnificent suit of shining copper armor, which he put on. Then he went into the garden and shook the bridle and the white horse appeared, already saddled. He put the bridle on the horse's head, jumped on its back and, just as the horse had told him, started to gallop madly about the garden, trampling everything in sight. The windows of the youngest daughter's bedroom overlooked the garden and she saw everything. As soon as the horse had destroyed all the flowers in

The windows of the youngest daughter's bedroom overlooked the garden and she saw everything.

the garden, the apprentice rode like a bolt of lightning to the church, handed the horse's reins to a man sitting outside, and went in, going straight to the altar where the priest anointed his head with holy oil. He turned and, bowing to everyone to his left and right, departed back down the aisle and went outside.

Everyone in the church was stunned at the spectacle of this noble stranger, even the Emperor himself, who remarked that he'd never seen anyone of such stately bearing in his entire life. Once outside the church, the apprentice remounted his horse and very quickly rode to the imperial garden, where he commanded the horse to restore all that had been destroyed. In a moment's time, the horse made everything even more beautiful than it was before. The young princess saw all this from her bedroom window, but said nothing.

Not long afterwards, another holy day arrived and again the Emperor went to church with his entire court. The youngest daughter pretended to be ill in order to stay home. Immediately, she went to her window overlooking the imperial garden. The gardener's apprentice removed from the second walnut a suit of silver armor, put it on, shook the bridle, and mounted the white horse, which appeared in the blink of an eye. Again they raced about the garden, trampling everything even more thoroughly than before. They then proceeded to the church. At the church, he did precisely what he'd done the first time. Then they returned to the garden and, upon command, the horse restored it even more beautifully than before. The youngest daughter observed everything. Upon their return, her two sisters told her again of the mysterious and handsome young stranger who appeared at church. She listened to all they had to say, but didn't reply with a single word.

On the next important holy day, the Emperor went to the church again with all of his servants and courtiers. Again the young daughter feigned illness to remain at home. This time, the apprentice drew from the third walnut a magnificent suit of golden armor.

Upon their return, her two sisters told her again of the mysterious and handsome young stranger who appeared at church.

After putting it on, he mounted the horse, trampled the garden, and, just as before, went to church. Returning to the ruined garden, he commanded the horse to make it three times as beautiful as before. The Emperor's daughter saw everything from her window and didn't say a word.

When they returned from church, the Emperor and every single soul who had been there told the young daughter of the marvel they had witnessed. The young daughter heard all that they said, but only laughed silently to herself. The gardener, when he beheld the extraordinary garden, rubbed his old eyes, for he could not believe what he was seeing. Was this his garden, or another one that had fallen out of heaven? He asked the apprentice what had happened. But the apprentice said that nothing had happened. He'd done only what his master, the gardener, had taught him. The garden was so magnificent that, when the Emperor saw it, he awarded the old gardener a large bag filled with gold coins.

Was this his garden, or another one that had fallen out of heaven?

The Suitors

As time passed, the Emperor remembered the three bouquets of flowers and spoke with the Queen about how they might find their daughters husbands. The moment the availability of his daughters was made known, suitors began arriving from other kingdoms to claim their hands. The eldest and middle daughters each chose a handsome prince, got married, and departed with their new husbands. But the youngest daughter rejected every suitor. What was the poor Emperor to do? He consulted with his councillors. It was decided that the young princess would be seated in a small tower near the imperial garden and that she would be given a gilded apple. All of the princes and noblemen from other kingdoms would pass in procession under the tower. The princess would throw the apple at the one she desired to marry. And so it was done.

First, all of the princes passed in front of her. She rejected them all. Then the noblemen passed before her, but she didn't even consider throwing the apple at any of them. Every young man, both good and bad, passed by—even the commoners! But she didn't look at any of them. She just stood there in the tower, holding the golden apple so tightly that it hurt her hand.

Now it so happened that the gardener's apprentice came into sight in the garden as he went about his work. The moment she saw him, the young princess hurled the apple and struck him squarely on the head. The princes and the noblemen were flabbergasted. The Emperor said that it had surely been a mistake, and he once again invited all of the princes and all of the nobility to pass by the tower. They passed by, each and every one, and again the young princess didn't so much as lean in their direction. Then they asked the bald gardener's apprentice to pass by again, and as he did she threw the apple and hit him in the head a second time. The Emperor was unable to accept that his daughter would choose someone of such a lowly state. And so he invited everyone

The moment she saw him, the young princess hurled the apple and struck him squarely on the head.

to pass a third time. And a third time the bald gardener's apprentice was struck on the head with the gilded apple which the young princess threw.

At this point, the Emperor, having no other recourse, gave his daughter's hand to the apprentice and, cursing their union, chased them both from the palace grounds. They departed from his sight with tears in their eyes. In a far corner of the Emperor's realm, they found a miserable underground hovel that, once upon a time had been a stable, and they decided to live there. But the princess recalled all of the things her husband had done in the garden and she urged him to summon his horse. The apprentice did as his wife desired: he summoned his horse and immediately commanded him to create an underground palace that had no equal on earth. The horse, without delay, made a magnificent palace containing precious treasures of such perfect rarity that one could not find such things anywhere, not even in the palace of the Emperor.

They departed from his sight with tears in their eyes.

The horse, without delay, made a magnificent palace containing precious treasures....

The War

ater that year, the Emperor learned that another emperor had declared war on him. And so he asked for the help of his two sons-in-law, who arrived immediately and began making preparation for battle, boasting all the while of the great exploits they would soon accomplish in the field. The gardener's apprentice went to the Emperor and asked if he might go with them, for perhaps, he said, if fortune smiled upon him, he might be able to kill just a single one of the enemy. But the Emperor and the two other sons-in-law rebuffed him, saying that he should leave them in peace, as they had quite enough to worry about without dragging a pathetic bald apprentice along into battle. But the bald apprentice persisted and finally, just to get rid of him, they gave him a rusty old sword and a horse that was so ancient its belly nearly touched the ground. But the gardener's apprentice happily mounted the old nag and departed. When he came to a marsh, he did as the white horse instructed and led the nag into a gigantic mudhole, in which they were soon quite stuck. When the Emperor passed, along with his two sons-in-law and his nobles, he made a show of trying to free the horse, but it was entirely in vain. The soldiers howled and cackled with laughter.

When everyone was at last out of sight, the apprentice again opened up the third walnut, put on his golden suit of armor, and removed the cow bladder from his head, freeing his long golden hair to fall across his back. He then shook the bridle and the horse arrived and told him all he must do when he faced the enemy in battle. When he came to the battlefield, riding on the white horse, he saw that the Emperor and his sons-in-law and all of his subjects were about to be vanquished by the enemy. He and the horse soared up into the sky over the battlefield to a height of three leagues. He then flew straight down, drew out his sword, and cut off the Emperor's small finger. He put this finger, which bore the imperial

He and the horse soared up into the sky over the battlefield to a height of three leagues.

ring, in his pocket. After this, he turned and fell upon the enemy, hacking at them with his sword as methodically as an experienced farmhand scythes a field of golden wheat.

Each time the enemy attempted to overtake him, he pulled on his horse's mane. Immediately, they shot like a lightning bolt up into the sky and then fell like a stone into the enemy's midst, slaying them on all sides. Three times he went into the sky and three times he fell back into the battle, touching down to earth like a howling tornado. Wherever he advanced, he piled the fallen enemy in great mountains. And he did it all in less time than it takes to tell this story.

In fact, the apprentice struck such terror into the hearts of the enemy that they began to flee, but he pursued them until there wasn't a single one in sight. On witnessing such extraordinary vigor, his father-in-law, the Emperor, was struck dumb. After the enemy had fled, he knelt where he was and thanked God for sending his angel, who had saved them from the hand of the enemy. Meanwhile, the apprentice had quickly returned to the mudhole, where he let his horse go and continued to try to pull the old nag out of the mud. When the Emperor passed by with his army, he was beaming with joy from the battle and, seeing the bald apprentice still struggling in the muck, he generously commanded his soldiers to help him out. When the apprentice arrived home, he told his wife the princess all that he'd done and her joy on hearing it knew no bounds.

The Milk of a Bird

Not long after the battle, the old Emperor lost his sight. All of the sorcerers assembled to give him their remedies. They placed large basins of water under the stars at night, so that the starlight could impart its magic, and then they brought this water to the Emperor to put upon his eyes. They recited long, complicated incantations both forwards and backwards. But everything they did only made matters worse. At last an astrologer, a powerful magician, was brought from a distant kingdom. He said the Emperor would not recover his sight unless he could bathe his eyes in the milk of the bird who lives on the other side of the River Jordan. The Emperor proclaimed that whoever succeeded in obtaining the milk of this bird would receive an imperial horse and half of his entire kingdom.

On hearing this, the two elder sons-in-law proposed that they would obtain this greatly needed milk. They mounted the best horses in the Emperor's stable, took a retinue of servants, and as much money as they were able to carry. They roamed the countryside, but were unable to find what they sought. Finally they came upon an old charlatan, one whose great quackery was known to everyone—even newborn infants just minutes out of their mothers' wombs knew of it—but the two sons-in-law were oblivious to it. They purchased from him a vial of ordinary cow's milk at an exorbitant price and returned to their father-in-law, leaping with joy.

At the same time, the Emperor's other son-in-law, the bald apprentice, had gone looking for the bird's milk as well. He shook his bridle, his horse appeared, and he explained how he needed to go to the other side of the River Jordan. "That will be easy, Master," the horse replied, "for that is precisely where I live." They procured the appropriate milk and returned, just as the other two sons-in-law were returning.

The two sons-in-law brought the vial of milk to the Emperor and he bathed his eyes with it as the astrologer had

They procured the appropriate milk and returned, just as the other two sons-in-law were returning.

prescribed. Nothing happened. He remained as blind as a dead bat. When the apprentice appeared with his vial of milk, which was in truth from the bird who lived on the other side of the River Jordan, the Emperor was at first unwilling to put any of it on his eyes. But at the behest of his wife, he agreed to try. As soon as he touched his eyes with it, he began to see somewhat as through a screen. He applied the milk a second time and saw better still. When he applied it a third time, he was able to see as well as anyone in the room. He was so overjoyed that he forgave everything he held in his heart against the bald apprentice.

Then the apprentice invited his father-in-law to visit him at home. When the Emperor arrived, he couldn't comprehend what his eyes saw. Fantastical treasures that did not exist in his own palace! The apprentice spoke. "Most excellent Emperor," he said, "I am the mysterious stranger who three times came to church." The Emperor was taken aback. The apprentice spoke a second time: "I am the one who transformed your imperial gardens into a botanical paradise." The Emperor could not believe what he was hearing, and his son-in-law spoke a third time: "And I am the one who saved you from the hand of the enemy in battle just as he was poised to vanquish you!" On hearing this last pronouncement, the Emperor's face turned white. When at last he had regained his color, he stammered, "How can you prove these things you tell me?"

At this, the young man stepped out of the room, took out the bridle and shook it. His horse appeared in a moment. He then took out the third walnut and drew from it his magnificent suit of golden armor, put it on, shook out his golden hair and arrayed it across his back, mounted his steed and reentered the room where his wife and father-in-law stood. "Behold, most excellent Emperor, the truth of what I have told you!" Then he pulled out the imperial ring, which he had taken from the Emperor's own finger, and gave it to the Emperor, who was thunderstruck beyond all reckoning. At this, the son-in-law spurred his horse and galloped around the grounds outside his palace like a blazing comet in the sky. His golden hair and armor shone as the very sun itself and the Emperor, who was watching, shaded his eyes lest he again go blind.

The Emperor was overcome with joy. He praised his daughter for choosing such a man, and tears came into her eyes. "Surely, loving father," she said, "you did not believe that I would ever have chosen someone of whom you would be ashamed." They embraced. And the Emperor, being now an old man, decided that very day to step down from his throne. He awarded it to his young son-in-law, who, together with his wife, ruled that kingdom in peace and happiness all the days of their lives.

He awarded it to his young son-in-law, who, together with his wife, ruled that kingdom in peace and happiness. . . .

A FLOWER LIST FROM THE GARDENS OF THE APPRENTICE

Alpine Currant

(*Ribes alpinum*) 3-4', Zone 2. Grown in bush form, produces a small red fruit that is edible. Also known as Mountain Currant.

Auricula Primrose

(*Primula auricula*) 8", Zone 3. A yellow-flowered Alpine primrose.

Chilicothe

(*Marah fubaccus*) 20', Tropical. This plant lives in the dry soils of southern California and Mexico. From a tall stem, the leaves grow with blades 2 to 4 inches wide. The flowers are cream-colored and cup-shaped and produce 2-inch-wide fruits.

Comfrey

(*Symphytum officinale*) 3', Zone 3. Introduced from Europe as a medicinal herb, it is now considered a weed in the U.S. This perennial blooms white to pink to purple.

Daffodil

(*Narcissus*) 3"-18", Zones 4-6. Popular garden bulbs forced in greenhouses for cut flowers. Hundreds of varieties, usually yellow with yellow, orange or white trumpets. Can be naturalized in garden, usually planted in groups of a dozen or more. Blooms from early spring to early summer.

Date palm

(Phoenix dactylifera) 100',
Zone 9. A subtropical plant
grown in parts of Arizona
and California that pro-
duces a brown, sweet fruit.
One of the oldest crops,
cultivation started over
5,000 years ago.

Dracena

(Cordyline terminalis) 12",
Zone 10. A tropical plant
with graceful sword-shaped
leaves, often grown as a
houseplant.

Epiphyte

A plant usually growing
on another plant. It has
aerial roots, none that
reach the ground, so it
derives its nutrients only
from air and rain.

Feather vine

(Ipomoea quamoclit) An
annual tropical vine which
has naturalized in southern
U.S. It produces slender,
tube-shaped red flowers
that bloom from late sum-
mer to early fall.

Fern

This family of plants has
grown on Earth for mil-
lions of years. They grow
from the tropics to near the
Arctic Circle. Like to grow
in cool, moist spots. Have
large lacy fronds or leaves.

Grapes

(Vitis) A vine highly
prized for its fruit which
are white or red or purple
and grows in clusters. It
prefers growing in a sunny
spot with well-drained soil.

Guinea chestnut flower
(*Pachira aquatica*) 15'-60',
Zone 10. A small tree with
spiny leaves. Small tubular
flowers are white to pink to
purple.

Hawkweed

(*Pilosella aurantiaca*) 20",
Zone 3. Also known as the
Devil's Paint-brush, a trou-
blesome common perennial
weed in North America
introduced from Europe.

Blooms with orange-red
heads one inch across at the
end of a long spike.

Hellebore

(*Helleobros viridis*) 2', Zone
6. Native to Europe, naturalized in the eastern U.S.
Flowers are yellowish-
green.

Hollyhock

(*Alcea rosea*) 10', Zones 2-3.
Biennial, lobed leaves,

blooms the second year in
many colors—yellow, red,
white, pink. Common
garden flower.

Hyacinth

(*Hyacinthus orientalis*) 18",
Zone 6. Grown from bulbs,
chiefly from Holland, in
many colors and sizes. Can
be grown outdoors as far
north as southern New
England, but often used for
forcing during winter.
Extremely fragrant.

Iris

(Iridaceae) 3"-4', Zones 3-7.
Perennial bulbs with
sword-like leaves and love-
ly, frilly flowers. Most
bloom from spring to early
summer.

Ivy

(Hedera) Zone 5-9. Ever-
green, clinging vines grown
in U.S. as houseplants and
in gardens. They climb by
attaching small root-like
appendages to walls.

Jacob's-rod

(Asphodeline lutea) 3'-4',
Zone 7. Commonly known
as Jacob's-rod, a member of
the Lily family, native to
the Mediterranean, pro-
duces fragrant yellow
flowers.

Liana

A woody, climbing or twin-
ing plant of the tropical
rainforest that roots in the
ground (as opposed to an
epiphyte).

Marsh Marigold

(Caltha palustris) 1'-3',
Zone 3. Also known as
cowslip, a pretty plant of
the swamps of Canada and
south to Iowa. Heart-
shaped leaves and yellow
flowers. It blooms in April
and then dies back to the
ground in mid-summer.

Magnolia

A conspicuous flowering
tree with white or pink fragrant flowers. It ranges
from a large shrub to a 90-

foot tree. Some can be grown in all but coldest zones in U.S. Blooms from early spring to mid-summer. Some are native to the Americas, others were brought here from Asia.

Orchid

Thousands of species and many hybrids make up this group of plants. The Cattleyas, the most popular of all orchids, feature the large lavender corsage orchid. Many orchids grow in the tropics of South America and Asia, but some, like the Lady Slipper, grow in the northern U.S.

Papaya

(Carica) 30', Zone 10. Popular fruit tree native to tropical America. The tree is succulent and short-lived. The fruit is a fleshy, melon-sized berry. Leaves are two feet long, deeply lobed and flowers are tubular, yellow. Also known as Pawpaw.

Peony

(Paeonia) 2'-5', Zones 3-5. A long-lived, very hardy perennial with huge showy blossoms, often fragrant. The blooms are white to pink to deep red.

Poinsettia

(Euphorbia pulcherrima) 12', Zone 9. Grown outdoors in subtropical gardens, does best in full sun. Native to Central America. A greenhouse plant in the North. The outer leaves are evergreen and bright red inner leaves form around the small yellow flowers.

Pomegranate

(*Punica*) 12'-20'. A shrub or small deciduous tree grown in the southern U.S. Large bright orange flowers produce 3-4 inch fruits that are bright red. Ruby red seeds inside make a wonderful juice.

Silver calice

(*Aechmea fusciata*) Zone 9. This houseplant from tropical America has long spine-edged leaves that grow from the center of the root. Red and yellow flowers spike up from the center in late summer to early fall.

Snake plant

(*Sanseviera trifasciata*) 1'-4', Zone 10. Sometimes known as Mother-in-law's Tongue. Leaves are tall, erect, and deep green with transverse sections of lighter green. Flowers are fragrant and pale green, although seldom blooms. Grown as houseplants, don't need much sun.

Sumac

(*Rhus*) 3'-30', Zones 2-6. Sumacs are suckering shrubs which grow well in poor soil. The leaves turn orange to deep red in the fall. The fruits are clusters of red berries that stay in an upright position all winter.

Tobacco plant

(*Nicotiana*) 1'-6'. Mostly grown as an annual. Member of the Nightshade family, N. tabacum's leaves are used for tobacco. Other plants in family are grown as colorful garden plants with trumpet-shaped blooms in red, white, rose, and purple.

Tulip

(Tulipa) 6"-24". Most are Zone 4. Very popular garden flowers grown from bulbs. Native to Europe and Near East. The largest number of tulip bulbs are imported to U.S. from the Netherlands. Tulips bloom in spring in a wide range of colors and usually produce a single cup-shaped flower.

Water-lily

(Nymphaea) This species is divided into hardy water-lilies that can overwinter in northern waters if their roots are below ice level and tropical water-lilies which need warm water to survive. Flowers of hardy type usually float on the water, while those in the tropics are supported on stems. The leaves of the water-lily float on the water and often look like big green plates. They can vary in size from 3 inches across to 6 feet.

Weeping willow

(Salix) Large group of deciduous plants which includes both trees and shrubs. There are six willows that can be considered "weeping" willows. The most common is the Babylon Weeping Willow, but it is only hardy in Zone 6. The hardiest is the Golden Weeping Willow (Zone 2), which has yellow branches.

Yucca

Zones 2-8. Member of the Agave family. Most species have no stem, just succulent, sword-like leaves ending in a point. A flower stalk rises out of the middle with white to pale green to pink waxy flowers.

Flowers In My Garden

Common name	Latin name	Date planted	Date divided

Common name	Latin name	Date planted	Date divided

Common name	Latin name	Date planted	Date divided

Common name	Latin name	Date planted	Date divided

Common name	Latin name	Date planted	Date divided

Common name	Latin name	Date planted	Date divided

Common name	Latin name	Date planted	Date divided

The reconciliation

The marshes

The battlefield

The underground palace

Talking with the gardener

The nymphs' house

The sorcerer's house

His house